"Graceology without feeling offer fresh perspectives on life, making you think about deeper questions in a way that feels approachable and open. If you're curious about the bigger picture but not sure where to start, this book offers an inviting and thoughtful place to begin. Uplifting and engaging, it speaks to the heart without overwhelming the mind."

Abigail Tiefenthaler, Co-Founder
Savvy Sales Strategy, eWomen Knoxville Managing Director

"Stories are interwoven into the fabric of every culture, every family, every person. Throughout time, stories have encouraged, inspired, and even challenged us to see beyond something greater than ourselves. No one was a better storyteller than Jesus. Whether he was with an individual or crowd, he was a master at inviting them into a greater journey and meaning though parables —stories with a spiritual lesson.

Likewise, Libby Jason masterfully invites us into this book of stories that help us find grace in the ordinary, the hard, the unforeseen, and the curious. In this, we are challenged to be the hands and feet of Jesus as our story, and His Story, is tethered to those we encounter in this journey of life."

Dr. JJ Jones, Pastor of Groups
Fellowship Bible Church, Brentwood, TN

"Libby Jason has written a wonderfully insightful book that will help you understand the amazing grace that God demonstrates to us every day. You will love the stories and even more, you will love the impact they have on you and your relationship with Christ!"

"Libby Jason's book is a perfect reminder that God broke the mold when he created each of us. It has been said "be yourself, everyone else is taken"—that's exactly what He had in mind as our heavenly personal stylist. Knowing who God is and who he says we are — is the ultimate confidence builder. I highly recommend this book for anyone who wants a greater understanding of grace and a greater appreciation of themselves— just exactly how they were created!"

"You can't help but be affected by Libby's brightness of spirit when you are with her. Her positive energy is joyfully contagious!"

"Libby takes her elegant styling skills to help women see their worth through the Lens of God's word. Her graceful storytelling will leave a lasting impression & remind you what your true identity looks like."

Donna Johnson, Entrepreneur & Bestselling Author
My Mentor Walks on Water and *My Mentor's Radical Love*

LIBBY JASON

grace
OLOGY

SIMPLE STORIES
for the
CURIOUS
SOUL

Published by HigherLife Development Services, Inc.
PO Box 623307
Oviedo, Florida 32762
(407) 563-4806
www.ahigherlife.com

ISBN: 978-1-964081-25-0 Paperback
ISBN: 978-1-964081-26-7 eBook

Library of Congress Case Number 1-14211140261

I dedicate this book to Seekers, that they may discover the grace and hope they are searching for and for Believers, so they may share the gospel.

May you grasp how wide and long and high and deep is the Father's love for you.

ACKNOWLEDGEMENTS

To the hundreds of women I have had the pleasure to style, to be a part of your most intimate longings, deep conversations and desire for self-worth. I am grateful to have shared in your journey and it is because of you, I have created this book.

To my publishers, graphic artists, copy editors and all who have worked tirelessly to bring this book to fruition, I thank you.

To my family, your support means everything to me. To my son, Austin, your creative talent inspires me, even though your work isn't in this book, I am always in awe of your artistic gift. To my son, Garrett, I trust that your dicerning mind and tender heart will find value, love, and hope in the words of this book. And to my husband, William, my constant source of encouragement—thank you for always standing by me, no matter my many endeavors!

TABLE OF CONTENTS

INTRODUCTION

As a wardrobe stylist, I've noticed that most women have a disconnect or dissatisfaction with their bodies—they may not dislike their looks, but they can't help feeling that they could look better or be thinner, prettier, etc. As a woman, I get that.

But have you considered that maybe, just maybe, a key to having a better relationship with yourself—a better sense of your own identity and worth—can be found in having a better relationship with your creator—the One who made you in the first place, the One who designed you and created a unique, one-of-a-kind identity for you?

Read on if you are even the slightest bit curious to learn more about why you were created and what your Heavenly Stylist had in mind when He created you and knit you together in your mother's womb. Perhaps these short stories will give you some helpful morsels of "truth chocolate" and insight to chew on. And perhaps they will guide you to understand how God's grace—and your intentional acceptance of that grace—can lead you to a stronger identity, a source of comfort and wisdom, and a strong sense of hope that surpasses all human understanding.

What is God's grace?

It is His unmerited favor He bestows on us because He loves us and wants reconciliation with us. Grace is the essence of God's character. It is His act of forgiving us and blessing us abundantly, in spite of the fact that we do not deserve to be treated so well. We do not earn grace; God bestows it on us, as stated in 2 Timothy 1:9 (NIV): "He has saved us and called us to a holy life—not because of anything we have done but because of his own purpose and grace. This grace was given to us in Christ Jesus before the beginning of time."

Imagine grace as the ultimate makeover—but for your soul. It's like walking into a high-end boutique, expecting to pay a fortune, only to find that everything has been paid for in advance.

Grace is a gift so extravagant, so unexpected, that it can leave us feeling a bit stunned. It's not about what we deserve or have earned. It's about being offered love, acceptance, and a fresh start, no strings attached. Throughout this book, we'll explore how this concept of grace can transform how we see ourselves and interact with the world around us.

It's a journey of discovery that might just change everything—and you're invited along for the ride!

Although the short but symbolic stories in this book are an intimate study of grace, they are much more about the character of God. The eight simple stories and the interactive exercise that follow all demonstrate the power of God's grace in our lives, if only we will accept it.

CHAPTER 1

THE UNDERCURRENT

surrender

R yan was the picture of confidence. His years of life-guarding had made him feel invincible in the water. Mike, less sure of himself, trusted in his friend's experience. One day, despite the warning red flag, they ventured into the waves for a carefree day at the beach.

At first, everything seemed fine. The friends rode wave after wave, laughing and enjoying the thrill. But slowly, imperceptibly, they drifted farther from shore. Then, without warning, the current shifted.

Imagine the sudden panic as both men realized they were in trouble. The ocean, which had been their playground moments ago, now threatened to become their grave. Mike surfaced, gasping for air, and looked around frantically for Ryan. But his friend was nowhere to be seen.

Below the surface, Ryan was facing a stark reality. All his skill, all his training, all his confidence—none of it mattered now. He was drowning, and no amount of fighting could save him.

Just when all seemed lost, hope arrived in the form of a nearby scuba-diving boat. They pulled Mike to safety and, hearing about Ryan, immediately sent a diver to search for him.

Picture this: A skilled diver, equipped with life-giving air, reaches out to the drowning Ryan. But in his panic and disorientation, Ryan can't grasp the offered help. It's only when he stops fighting—when he surrenders to the rescuer—that he can receive the precious air he needs to survive.

Isn't this a powerful image of our relationship with God? So often, we're like Ryan—confident in our abilities, thinking we can handle life on our own. We ignore the warning signs and venture into dangerous waters. And when we find ourselves drowning in life's challenges, we often fight against the very help we need.

Like that diver, God always reaches out to us, offering the breath of life. But to receive it, we must stop fighting, stop trying to save ourselves, and surrender to His saving grace.

True strength comes from trusting and surrendering to God's grace rather than relying on our own abilities.

"God is our refuge and strength, an ever-present help in trouble."

Psalm 46:1 (NIV)

———— REFLECTIVE QUESTIONS ————

1. Can you recall a time when you felt confident in your abilities, only to find yourself suddenly overwhelmed? How did that experience change your perspective?

   _____

   _____

   _____

   _____

2. In what areas of your life do you tend to say, "I've got this" instead of turning to God for help? What might change if you invite God into those areas?

   _____

   _____

   _____

   _____

3. The Bible tells us, "Apart from me, you can do nothing" (John 15:5). How does this challenge or comfort you?

   _____

   _____

   _____

   _____

4. Ryan had to stop fighting to receive the life-saving air. In what ways might you be "fighting" against God's help in your life?

_____

_____

_____

_____

5. Acknowledging that God is like the diver, always ready to rescue us, what's holding you back from accepting His help?

_____

_____

_____

_____

Remember, just as Ryan's swimming skills couldn't save him from the powerful undercurrent, our own abilities and strengths often fall short as we navigate life's challenges. But there's hope—God is always there, ready to rescue us if we're willing to let go and trust Him.

CHAPTER 2

HOPE IN THE MIRROR

identity

Have you ever stood in front of a mirror and felt completely disheartened by what you saw? That's where we find Susan scrutinizing her reflection with a critical eye: "If only I were thinner, prettier, younger," she thinks. "If only…"

Life has been throwing Susan curveballs lately. Between juggling the demands of teenage children and a husband often away for work, she has been existing on quick snacks and stress. Now, faced with dressing up for a company event, she feels overwhelmed. "Nothing fits!" she exclaims through tears. "I look so frumpy!" and "I am so overweight!"

Susan's habit of pointing out her flaws runs deep. It's as ingrained as the lies she's heard so often: "You're not good enough. No one cares. You're not important." These words have become the lens through which she sees herself, giving power to her mirror, her neighbors, her friends, and even her family to define who she is.

From the outside, Susan's childhood looked picture-perfect. But behind closed doors, chaos reigned. Her mother's struggle with alcohol left Susan walking on eggshells, never knowing what she'd find when she came home. Despite hearing "I love you" from her parents, loneliness, fear, anxiety, and shame were her constant companions.

"Maybe if I were smarter, more obedient, and worked harder, my mom would see me, value me, and hopefully stop drinking," Susan would think. She spent her life trying to earn love, to be whatever anyone needed her to be. When asked about her feelings, Susan couldn't even begin to answer. Numbness and complacency had become her closest friends.

Comparison ruled Susan's life. Her people-pleasing behavior led her to believe everyone else's opinions, needs, and desires were far more important than her own. Susan had no idea who she truly was. She'd heard the phrase "Just be yourself" and thought, "Who is that? Where is my identity?"

But one day, a friend asked her a question that would change everything: "Susan, what stirs inside you when you hear that you are God's workmanship? Do you know you are truly loved, wanted, and created with a purpose?"

How could that be? Susan had spent her whole life feeling not good enough. How could God value her and have a purpose for her? How could He love her simply for being herself?

The answer lay in God's love for His creation. Susan began to reflect on the years she had given to past voices, associations, and thoughts to define her identity. This God she had heard about seemed safe and trustworthy. Perhaps His words over her—telling her she was loved, wanted, created, and free—were her true identity.

At that moment, Susan began to see a glimmer of hope. Maybe, just maybe, there was more to her story than what she saw in the mirror. Maybe her worth wasn't determined by her appearance, her accomplishments, or others' opinions. Maybe, in God's eyes, she was not invisible and through his love and grace she was already enough.

The deep truth is that we are intricately and purposefully made by God, even when we struggle with feelings of inadequacy.

"I will give thanks to You, for I am fearfully and wonderfully made; wonderful are your works and my soul knows it very well."

Psalm 139:14 (NASB)

───── REFLECTIVE QUESTIONS ─────

1. Can you relate to Susan's struggle with self-image? In what ways have you allowed other people or circumstances to define your worth?

   _____

   _____

   _____

   _____

2. How might your life change if you genuinely believed you are loved, wanted, and created with a purpose by God?

   _____

   _____

   _____

   _____

3. What "mirrors" in your life have you given power to define who you are? How can you start to see yourself through God's eyes instead?

   _____

   _____

   _____

   _____

4. Susan's friend asked her a powerful question about God's view of her. Who in your life might need to hear a similar message of hope and value?

    _____

    _____

    _____

    _____

5. If you could rewrite the story of your identity, starting today, what would you want it to say? How can God's love for you shape this new narrative?

    _____

    _____

    _____

    _____

CHAPTER 3

SARAH'S REDEMPTIVE OFFER

grace and mercy

S arah's heart raced as she sat in the stark, silent courtroom. The weight of her choices pressed down on her, each mistake a heavy stone in her pocket, dragging her deeper into despair. She had always tried to be a good person, hadn't she? But looking back, her life's path seemed littered with missteps, broken promises, and moments of weakness she couldn't take back.

The judge's gavel echoed like thunder, and Sarah flinched. Her name rang out, a death knell in the hushed room. On trembling legs, she approached the bench, feeling the eyes of unseen accusers burning into her back.

As the list of her transgressions unfurled, Sarah's world crumbled. Each charge struck her heart: lies she'd told to protect herself, people she'd hurt out of anger or fear, opportunities squandered, love rejected. The litany seemed endless. How had she strayed so far from the person she'd always imagined herself to be?

Tears streamed down Sarah's face as shame engulfed her. She wanted to disappear, to sink into the floor and fade away. What was the point of it all if this was where she ended up— alone, afraid, and utterly without hope?

But then...

The judge's expression softened, his eyes meeting hers with unexpected warmth. He descended from the bench, his robe rustling as he approached. Sarah tensed, bracing for the final blow. Instead, the judge did something extraordinary—he sat beside her.

"Sarah," he said, his voice gentle yet firm, "I see you. I see your struggles, your pain, your regret. And I'm offering you a choice."

Sarah looked up, confusion mingling with a tiny spark of hope.

"Someone is willing to stand in your place," the judge continued. "To bear the weight of everything that brought you here today. He believes in your worth, even when you can't see it yourself. His name is Jesus."

Sarah's mind reeled. It didn't make sense. Why would anyone do that for her? How could there be a way out when she'd dug herself in so deep?

"I...I don't understand," she whispered.

The judge smiled. "You don't have to understand it all right now. You just have to decide if you're willing to accept this gift. To believe that you are worthy of a second chance, of love beyond measure."

Sarah closed her eyes, feeling the tug-of-war between cynicism and a desperate longing to believe. Could it be this simple? This profound?

When she opened her eyes again, the courtroom had changed. The oppressive silence was replaced by a feeling of possibility, of a door cracking open to reveal a glimpse of light.

Sarah took a deep breath. For the first time in longer than she could remember, she felt the stirring of something new, something that felt suspiciously like...hope.

Even when we struggle with guilt, God's grace assures us that we are not condemned but fully loved and accepted in Christ.

"Therefore there is now no condemnation for those who are in Christ Jesus."

Romans 8:1 (NASB)

————— REFLECTIVE QUESTIONS —————

1. What emotions did Sarah's journey through the court-room evoke in you? Have you ever felt a similar weight of regret or shame?

_____

_____

_____

_____

2. The judge's offer seems too good to be true. What makes it difficult for us to accept unconditional love or forgiveness?

_____

_____

_____

_____

3. What thoughts or fears might hold you back from accepting the judge's offer if you were in Sarah's position?

_____

_____

_____

_____

4. The story speaks of someone willing to "stand in your place." What might this look like in everyday life outside a legal context? Have you ever experienced someone taking on your burdens?

    _____

    _____

    _____

    _____

5. Sarah's story ends with a spark of hope. What does hope mean to you? Can you recall a time when hope appeared in an unexpected place in your own life?

    _____

    _____

    _____

    _____

6. The judge says Sarah doesn't have to understand everything to accept the gift. How do you feel about embracing something you can't fully explain or comprehend?

    _____

    _____

    _____

    _____

CHAPTER 4

THE PERFECT DATE

relationship

Have you ever met someone who just seemed to radiate joy? That's how Brad felt about Alicia. They were co-workers, but there was something special about her that drew him in. Brad thought he knew Alicia, but did he really?

It's funny how we can think we know someone when we've barely scratched the surface, isn't it?

Curiosity got the better of Brad, and he took a leap of faith, asking Alicia to go out for coffee. As they chatted over steaming cups, he began to uncover the layers of who Alicia really was—her background, her family, her journey to their shared workplace. With each date, Brad discovered more—her likes, dislikes, attitude, and, most importantly, her character.

As their relationship deepened, something beautiful happened. They started sharing their innermost feelings, thoughts, and desires. Brad found himself in a place he'd never been before—a place of trust and understanding. Alicia "got" him because she'd been there, too. She had felt the same grief, heartbreak, temptations, joy, hope, and even anger. You know, the kind of anger we usually keep hidden away.

Their conversations grew longer and deeper. Brad found himself thinking of Alicia often, wondering what would make her smile or how she'd react in different situations. He began to see life through her eyes. They talked for hours, spending more and more time together. And something amazing started to happen: Brad noticed changes in himself. His character was improving, and he liked the person he was becoming. His heart felt most alive when connected with Alicia's.

This is what a deep relationship looks like. It's beautiful, isn't it? But here's the thing—as wonderful as human relationships can be, they're not perfect. There will always be flaws, disagreements, and disappointments because, well, we're human.

But what if I told you there's someone who offers a perfect relationship? Someone who knows you inside and out, understands your deepest fears and greatest hopes, and loves you unconditionally? That someone is Jesus.

You see, we can know about Jesus, or we can truly know Him. Just like Brad went from knowing about Alicia to really knowing her, we can have that same journey with Jesus. We can be fully ourselves with Him and feel completely safe. We have no fear of being vulnerable because His love is pure and perfect. Jesus isn't looking for religious rituals or dutiful compliance. He's longing for an honest, deep relationship with us.

And the best part? We don't have to change or pretend to be someone we're not. He loves us just as we are.

God's perfect grace and love give us the freedom to be vulnerable and open without fear or anxiety because His love is safe and complete. There is trust and safety in God's goodness, much like the security that comes with truly being known in a relationship.

"There is no fear in love. But perfect love drives out fear because fear has to do with punishment."

John 4:18 (NIV)

─────── REFLECTIVE QUESTIONS ───────

1. Think about a time when you went from knowing about someone to truly knowing them. What changed in that relationship? How did it affect you?

   _____

   _____

   _____

   _____

2. What makes you feel safe enough to share your true self with someone? Is there a person who comes to mind when you think about this kind of trust?

   _____

   _____

   _____

   _____

3. If you could have a conversation with Jesus right now, what would you want to tell Him? What do you think He might say to you?

   _____

   _____

   _____

   _____

4. How might your life change if you approached your relationship with Jesus like Brad approached his relationship with Alicia—with curiosity, openness, and a desire to know Him more deeply?

_____

_____

_____

_____

5. What's holding you back from pursuing a deeper relationship with Jesus? What step could you take today to get to know Him better?

_____

_____

_____

_____

Remember, just as Brad's relationship with Alicia transformed him, a relationship with Jesus has the power to change us from the inside out. He's inviting you into a love story far more significant than any earthly romance—a story in which you're fully known and perfectly loved.

How do you start? You ask!

"Ask and it will be given to you; seek and you will find; knock and the door will be opened to you. For everyone who asks receives; the one who seeks finds; and to the one who knocks, the door will be opened."

Matthew 7:7–8 (NIV)

CHAPTER 5

THE UMBRELLA

sin

The rain was relentless, pouring down in sheets and blowing sideways. I had a hoodie on, thinking it would be enough, but nothing could protect me like an oversized umbrella could.

Imagine the rain as God's wrath and the umbrella as Jesus. Sin is who I am. The umbrella shields sinful me, protecting me from God's wrath. Let's break that down.

Before we can see our need for the Good News (the cure for our sinful nature), we must understand the bad news. A common worldview is that people are basically good. But the Bible says, "There is no one who does good, not even one" (Rom. 3:12). And Romans 3:23 says, "For all have sinned and fall short of the glory of God."

So, what does the word "sin" mean?

Sin is opposite of holiness. "Sin" originally comes from an archery term, meaning to miss the mark. Whether you miss by a little or a lot, a miss is a miss. There's no such thing as "almost."

God, as the creator of life, allows us to choose freely and willingly.

When Adam and Eve chose disobedience, they unleashed sin into the world, and since then, every human is born separated from God. Sin became the barrier, forfeiting our privileged position with a perfect God.

God's wrath is not arbitrary; it's a consequence of His perfect nature. Being holy and just, He can't overlook sin. There's no "I knew you meant well, so it's okay." Justice demands a consequence, and it affects our eternity.

We can't achieve perfection. Have I ever lied, made a mistake, taken something that wasn't mine, spoken harshly, or been apathetic toward God's gift? All the above!

By my human nature, I have missed the mark.

How can I reconcile with God and have an eternal relationship if sin is in the way? There has to be another way.

That way is Jesus. Without Jesus, we would be subject to God's wrath. Jesus became the umbrella.

My personal repentance began when I truly understood what Jesus did for me. He forgave my apathy toward His ultimate gift—His life. Once I trusted in Him, my past no longer mattered. There is no condemnation with Christ. This is true freedom!

Do I still mess up? Absolutely! But now, through repentance, it's not just a change of heart; it's a heart change. I have an advocate, the Holy Spirit, who intercedes for me, strengthens my character, aligns me with God's plan, and serves as my comforter and eternal advisor. Every day, I get a new beginning.

Imagine driving down a road and hearing there's a disaster ahead. Would you keep driving? Or would you turn around and take a safe, sure route to your final destination?

A true heart turnaround is repentance.

Through repentance, we receive God's grace, forgiveness, and refreshing cleansing.

Even in our wandering, God longs to extend grace and compassion to us when we turn back to Him in repentance.

"If we confess our sins, He is faithful and just and will forgive us our sins and purify us from all unrighteousness."

1 John 1:9 (NIV)

"Yet the Lord longs to be gracious to you; therefore He will rise up to show you compassion. For the Lord is a God of justice. Blessed are all who wait for Him!"

Isaiah 30:18 (NIV)

————— REFLECTIVE QUESTIONS —————

I. What value do you see in the umbrella?

_____

_____

_____

_____

2. What is repentance? It's a true change of heart toward God.

_____

_____

_____

_____

When we understand the protection Jesus offers, we see the value in turning toward Him. We realize that, like the umbrella shielding us from the storm, Jesus shields us from what we deserve and offers us a new path, a new beginning, and an eternal relationship with God. This is God's Grace toward us.

CHAPTER 6

ON THE COURTS
fellowship

Betsy had heard whispers about pickleball for years. She had dabbled in tennis, volleyball, and even golf, but none of these sports truly captured her interest. Yet something about this new sport intrigued her enough to sign up for a lesson. To her surprise, pickleball was not only fun but also accessible, with a bunch of friendly faces her age just starting out.

After a few weeks, Betsy began gathering some of the other players. They practiced techniques, ran drills, studied the rules, and celebrated their best shots together. The atmosphere was always one of encouragement and a shared desire to improve.

Betsy wasn't naturally competitive, but she had a strong drive to achieve her "personal best." She found a sense of community among the players, each striving to apply what they learned and become better. They shared a common goal: to improve their game while having fun.

In sports, we can be spectators watching the game, or we can be players. Attending church is a lot like joining a community of players and getting involved. We call it "fellowship." People come with their unique life experiences to a place where they can feel accepted and learn how to apply spiritual teachings to their lives, striving to reflect

Jesus's character. It's a place where we can share our struggles and our victories, building connections with others.

We weren't meant to journey through life alone; we need community to thrive.

Is there a perfect church? No, because churches are made up of imperfect people. Yet we come together for a shared purpose: to know Jesus better and to spread His Good News.

We are to encourage one another in faith and worship. There is biblical importance of fellowship, community, and the truth that we are not meant to walk through this life alone or in isolation. Community strengthens us, and God's grace supports our belonging to Him and to each other.

"And let us consider how
we may spur one another
on toward love and good
deeds, not giving up meeting
together, as some are in
the habit of doing, but
encouraging one another-and
all the more as you see the
Day approaching."

Hebrews 10:24–25 (NIV)

————— REFLECTIVE QUESTIONS —————

1. Do you attend church, or are you actively involved
   in one? If you're just attending, what holds you back
   from getting involved?

   _____
   _____
   _____
   _____
   _____

2. What has your experience with churches been like in
   the past?

   _____
   _____
   _____
   _____
   _____

3. What are you seeking in a church community?

   _____
   _____
   _____
   _____
   _____

Just as Betsy found her niche on the pickleball court, you, too can find your place within a church community, where growth, support, and joy await. It's called "fellowship," and it is essential for every human being.

CHAPTER 7

THE SOLID CHAIR

trust

Nancy, standing at a petite 5'2", often found herself in a predicament in her own kitchen. The top shelves were always just out of reach, mocking her every time she needed something stored up high. One particularly busy afternoon, she once again stretched on her tiptoes, fingers grasping air. Frustrated, she remembered a stool in the garage.

As she dragged the stool into the kitchen, she noticed one of its legs was loose. She tried tightening it, but it wouldn't budge. "Oh, I'll only be on it for a moment," she thought, brushing off the risk of danger. She placed her foot on the stool, and it wobbled precariously. Instinctively, she pulled back, her heart racing. That stool was a disaster waiting to happen.

Determined, Nancy scanned the room, and her eyes landed on a sturdy wooden chair. It was solid, firm, and had four stable legs—nothing loose, nothing wobbly. She knew without a doubt that it could support her weight. With a deep breath, she stepped up, reaching the top shelf effortlessly.

As Nancy retrieved her items, a thought struck her: "How often do we, in life, lean on the 'wobbly stools' of our own understanding and efforts?" We convince ourselves that our makeshift solutions will hold, only to find them crumbling beneath us.

In contrast, trusting God is like choosing a solid chair. We can depend on Him entirely, knowing He will never fail us. He is our Creator, who understands our needs far better than we do. Just as Nancy had to transfer her trust from the unreliable stool to the sturdy chair, we must learn to transfer our trust from our own unstable efforts to God's unwavering strength.

Trusting in God means acknowledging that He sees the whole picture when we see only a fragment. It means believing His plans are for our good, even when we don't understand them. It's like sitting down on a solid chair without a second thought because we trust it will hold us.

The following verse encourages full reliance on God's wisdom and guidance, trusting Him wholeheartedly. God's grace and faithfulness give us a solid foundation to place our trust in Him, especially in times of weakness, knowing His grace sustains us.

"Trust in the LORD with all your heart and lean not on your own understanding; in all your ways submit to Him, and He will make your paths straight."

Proverbs 3:5–6 (NIV)

─────── REFLECTIVE QUESTIONS ───────

1. What "wobbly stools" in your life have you been relying on? How have they proven to be unreliable?

_____

_____

_____

_____

2. Can you recall a time when trusting in God brought stability and peace into a situation?

_____

_____

_____

_____

3. What steps can you take to transfer your trust from your own efforts to God?

_____

_____

_____

_____

4. How does the analogy of the solid chair deepen your understanding of trusting in God?

_____

_____

_____

_____

Trusting in God is not just a one-time act; it's a daily decision to rely on His strength and wisdom over our own. Like Nancy with her solid chair, we can face life's challenges confidently, knowing that God's support is unwavering, and His love is steadfast. When we transfer our trust to Him, we find the firm foundation we need to navigate any situation.

CHAPTER 8

A MOTHER'S STORY

faith

Diana's journey of faith began like many others - with a sense of obligation. As a young girl, she found herself in church every Sunday, not out of personal desire, but to please her grandparents. It was a ritual, complete with polished patent leather shoes, pristine white gloves, and a mandatory head covering. The church, to Diana, was a place of formality and tradition, far removed from her everyday life.

But life has a way of shaking up our routines. When Diana's grandmother passed away, and her parents divorced, the Sunday morning ritual faded away. It might have been the end of Diana's church experience, but fate - or perhaps something more - had other plans.

As a teenager, Diana stumbled upon a local church offering a "folk music service." The draw? Well, if we're being honest, it wasn't a sudden spiritual awakening. It was a crush on the guitar player! But sometimes, the most profound journeys begin with the simplest of motivations.

What Diana found in this new church surprised her. Gone was the stiff formality of her childhood experiences. Instead, she discovered a casual atmosphere, a pastor with a sense of humor, and an approachability she had never associated with the church before. The idea that she could simply walk up to the pastor and have a conversation was revolutionary to her.

Excited by this new experience, Diana couldn't wait to share it with her mother. But her enthusiasm was met with skepticism. "Jesus is just a crutch," her mother said dismissively. "You should learn to take care of yourself." Despite this discouragement, something had sparked in Diana, and she continued to attend.

As she entered young adulthood, Diana found herself grappling with the big questions that we all face at some point. Why am I here? Where do I belong? She knew her parents loved her, but there was still an emptiness inside that she couldn't quite explain or fill.

Little did Diana know that these questions, this search for meaning, was the beginning of a much bigger journey. The casual church services, the approachable pastor, the questions she tucked away in her heart - all of these were small seeds being planted. Seeds that would one day grow into a faith that would transform her life in ways she couldn't yet imagine.

Diana's story reminds us that faith often begins in unexpected ways. It doesn't always start with a dramatic revelation or a lifelong commitment. Sometimes, it begins with a crush on a guitar player, a pastor who makes you laugh, or simply a place where you feel you can ask questions without judgment. And sometimes, it starts with a void - an emptiness that nothing else seems to fill.

As Diana continued to explore and question, she unknowingly took the first steps on a path that would lead her to discover a love and purpose beyond anything she had imagined. Her journey was just beginning, and the best was yet to come.

Faith is defined as a positive response we have to what God has already provided to us by grace. In other words, God provides grace to us, and we have to be intentional about accepting and receiving it. Salvation is a gift we receive by trusting in His grace, not by our own works.

"For it is by grace you have been saved, through faith-and this is not from yourselves, it is the gift of God-not by works, so that no one can boast."

Ephesians 2:8–9 (NIV)

────── REFLECTIVE QUESTIONS ──────

1. Have you ever felt an emptiness inside, even when you were surrounded by people who love you? What do you think might fill that void? Reflect on those moments of emptiness and consider what or who might fill that void in a lasting way.

_____

_____

_____

_____

2. Can you identify moments in your life when you tried to control everything around you? How did that work out for you? Think about times when you leaned on your own understanding and efforts. Did they lead to peace or frustration?

_____

_____

_____

_____

3. What does the idea of transferring your trust to God mean to you? Contemplate the metaphor of the solid

chair versus the wobbly stool. How can you apply this to your faith journey?

_____

_____

_____

_____

4. How does understanding the sacrifice of Jesus change your perspective on God's love for you? Reflect on the depth of God's love shown through Jesus's sacrifice. How does this impact your view of your worth and purpose?

_____

_____

_____

_____

If you find yourself searching, longing for a deeper connection, or struggling with the void in your heart, know this: God's love for you is immeasurable. He waits patiently for you to turn to Him, to transfer your trust from the unstable foundations of this world to His steadfast love. You don't have to have all the answers to take the next step. Simply open your heart and invite Him in. He is ready to walk this journey with you, filling your life with purpose, peace, and a love that surpasses all understanding.

CHAPTER 9

BLACK, RED, AND WHITE
interactive exercise

S ome people learn by reading, and some by hearing. Others are visual learners, and some learn best by doing. This interactive exercise is for everyone, but it will appeal especially to the doers. This illustration will help you understand the message of salvation in a hands-on way.

Materials Needed

Four body outlines—cutouts shaped like a human body—in black, red, white, and any other color.

Steps to Illustrate Salvation

1. The body outline:

Place the body outline that is not black, red, or white on the floor or a table in front of you. This represents a person—you, me, anyone.

2. The black figure:

Place the black figure over the body outline. The black represents sin. When we look at the body now, we see black. This signifies how sin covers us. When God looks at us in our natural state, He sees sin.

3. The red figure:

Next, place the red figure on top of the black one. The

red represents Jesus's blood shed for us. Notice the red figure is slightly larger than the black, signifying that His blood covers all our sins. It's a powerful reminder that no sin is too great to be covered by the sacrifice of Jesus.

4. The white figure:

Now place the white figure over the red one. The white represents Jesus Himself—pure, clean, and holy. This figure completely covers the others. When God looks at the body now, He only sees white. This means that through Jesus, we are seen as pure, clean, whole, and complete.

What This Means

- No sin: God no longer sees our sins.

- No stain: We are cleansed from our past mistakes.

- No condemnation: There is no judgment against us.

- Redeemed: We are bought back from the power of sin.

- Rescued: We are saved from the consequences of our wrongdoing.

- New creations: We are made new in Christ, with a fresh start.

Dear reader, this simple exercise carries a profound truth. Just as the white figure covers all the others, Jesus's sacrifice covers all our sins. When we accept Him as our personal Savior, God no longer sees our faults but sees us as spotless and pure because of Jesus.

Perhaps you've felt the weight of your own "black figure"—the sins and mistakes that seem to define you. Maybe you've tried to cover them with your own efforts, but nothing seems to work. The Good News is, you don't have to carry that burden alone. Jesus has already done the work for you. His blood has covered every sin, and He offers you a new beginning.

All it takes is a step of faith to accept His grace. Acknowledge your need for Him, believe in what He has done for you, and invite Him into your life.

──────   REFLECTIVE QUESTIONS   ──────

I.   What areas of your life feel covered in "black"? How have these areas impacted your relationship with God and others?

_____

_____

_____

_____

2.   Have you ever tried to cover your own sins with your efforts? How did that work out for you?

_____

_____

_____

_____

3.   What does it mean to you that Jesus's blood covers all your sins, no matter how great?

_____

_____

_____

_____

4. Are you ready to let Jesus's sacrifice redefine you, making you a new creation in God's eyes?

_____

_____

_____

_____

a prayer
for salvation

To accept Jesus Christ as your personal Lord and Savior and to invite Him into your life, pray the prayer on the next page.

The exact words are not as important as what's in your heart. Speak to God from the depths of your heart, and know you are heard.

This is your moment. Embrace the gift of salvation, and step into the new life God has prepared for you. You are loved, you are forgiven, you are free, and you are made new!

"Dear God, I know I am a sinner, and I need Your forgiveness. I believe that Jesus died for my sins and rose again. I want to turn from my sins and invite You into my heart and life. I want to trust and follow You as my Lord and Savior. Thank You for loving me, for covering my sins, and for making me a new creation. In Jesus' name, amen."

NEXT STEPS IN YOUR JOURNEY

If you have accepted God's grace and how it can enhance your life, relationships, and personal walk with God, here are three steps to take to continue your journey:

Get connected to a church: Finding a church home is crucial to your spiritual growth. You may have to attend several churches before finding one that feels like home. Remember, there are no perfect churches, but there is a community that is perfect for you.

Join a Bible study and life group: Connecting with a Bible study group and a "life group" will surround you with others who are also eager to grow in Christ. These smaller communities within the church will provide support, encouragement, and accountability on your journey.

Get a good study Bible: Investing in a good study Bible is essential for your personal spiritual development as a curious soul! A study Bible contains resources that can help you understand the content better, including notes, commentary, background information, historical context, insights into the meaning of a passage, and maps. Many churches have bookstores where you can find study Bibles; you also can ask for recommendations from your church leaders. A study Bible will help you understand the Scriptures more deeply and apply them to your life.

Moving Forward

Embracing your new faith journey and understanding "graceology" is a significant step. Here are some additional actions to consider taking as you grow in your relationship with God:

- Engage in regular prayer and devotion: Make time each day to pray and read your Bible. This daily habit will strengthen your faith and deepen your understanding of God's Word.

- Serve in your church: Find ways to get involved in your church community. Remember, don't be a spectator! Serving others is a practical way to live out your faith and make meaningful connections.

- Share your faith: Don't keep the joy and peace you've found to yourself. Share your story with others and be a light in their lives.

FINAL REFLECTION
Let Your Light Shine

Remember, this journey is not about perfection; it is about progress and growth in your relationship with God. Each step you take is a step toward a deeper, more fulfilling life in Christ. If you ever feel lost or unsure, return to the truth that God loves you, has redeemed you, and has a purpose for your life. Surround yourself with a supportive community, immerse yourself in God's Word, and trust in His plan for you.

Your new life in Christ is an adventure filled with hope, transformation, and endless possibilities. Embrace it fully, and let your story be a testament to God's amazing grace and love.

"Let your light shine before men, that they may see your good works and glorify your Father in heaven."

Matthew 5:16 (NIV)

This verse has always been my life verse because, no matter where life has taken me—whether working with women as a personal stylist or working in everyday, mundane jobs—my purpose has always been to reflect the grace of God, not my own abilities. I've wanted people to be curious, to notice something different in me, and to wonder, "Why does she have such a positive outlook?" or "How does she get through difficult times with such resilience?"

I've faced many challenges: illness, death of loved ones, abandonment, cancer, addiction in my family, financial ruin, and moments of deep loneliness. But through it all, I know that God sees me, every part of me. As I have leaned (depended) on Him, His grace has carried me through, and every trial has shaped me to become more like Christ.

When I first heard the news, "You have breast cancer," I was stunned. I had just gotten a physical, blood work, etc., and had received a so-called clean bill of health. The mammogram saved my life.

After the routine exams, labs, appointments, and loss of my hair, I decided I could go through this experience with disbelief, anger, or joy. I chose joy.

As a personal wardrobe stylist, I figured if I was going to have to go through chemotherapy, I was going to make it a fashion statement and give hope to other women.

First, I bought three wigs: a curly, highlighted full head of hair; a short, sleek straight bob; and a long red, sexy wig. My husband thought, "Oh, wow, three new women!" I also bought jewelry and makeup and refused to hide. Many months and years later, I was told my journey was a true inspiration for other women going through treatment. The mantra "Let your light shine" was paramount for me because it was by the grace of God I survived and could be an example of His joy to others.

During one of my chemotherapy sessions, I was barely holding it together and facing another round of IV treatments. But even then, I found myself asking, "Okay, God, who am I supposed to encourage today?"

And right there, He placed a "newbie" in the room—a woman arrived seeming incredibly scared and unsure. I was able to comfort her and share the light of Christ—a light born of His grace.

That's why Matthew 5:16 means so much to me. It's a reminder that in everything I do, it's never about me—it's about reflecting God's grace, His ultimate purpose in my life, inviting curiosity to those who want to know more about Him, and being a light to those around me.

ABOUT THE AUTHOR

Libby Jason is a passionate follower of Christ, a style expert, and an engaging author with a heart for helping women recognize their true worth. With more than two decades of experience in fashion, beauty, and business, she's made it her mission to show women that they are uniquely created with a message to share with the world. Through her work, Libby empowers women to step into confidence, embrace their visibility, and become leaders in their professions and communities.

A former co-owner of a fashion boutique in Newport Beach, California, Libby has a background in skin care and cosmetics. Her expertise has touched high-end clientele, including members of the entertainment industry, such as Destiny's Child, political figures, the staff of governors and senators, and sports figures. Her most recent styling work was featured on national television, on the TODAY show.

Libby believes that when women discover their value in God's eyes, they no longer feel invisible but instead step boldly into the spotlight. Whether she's speaking on stage, styling for a $7M client's MasterMind, or helping clients prepare for their next big event, Libby's approach is the same: to inspire confidence, cultivate self-worth, and reflect God's love in everything she does.

When she's not writing, styling, or playing pickleball, Libby is a devoted supporter of animal-rescue foundations and loves spending time with her dogs. She is married with two adult sons and lives in Franklin, Tennessee.

WORK WITH LIBBY

Experience our confidence-building styling sessions.

No more guesswork because your image and wardrobe will truly represent you, your lifestyle and personality.

 # SPEAKER ENGAGEMENTS

Hire Libby to speak at your next event!

Contact www.libbyjason.com for more information about these services.

THANK YOU FOR READING!

If you enjoyed this book, and feel others would benefit by reading it, please consider the following:

- Sharing or mentioning your thoughts about Graceology on Facebook, X, Instagram, Tic Toc, or other social media sites you use.

- Write a positive Review on Amazon.com, Goodreads, Barnes and Noble, or any other retailer sites that have a review system.

- Suggesting Graceology to Family and Friends. Share my website Link.

- Encourage Graceology at your Book Club or Woman's activity events.

- Purchase additional copies to give away as personal gifts.

To Order Bulk copies of Graceology, please visit LibbyJason.com and contact the author direct, or you can send an email to the publisher at: info@ahigherlife.com